MY DADDY LIKES TO SAY

It's A Dogs Life

By DENISE BRENNAN-NELSON
Illustrated by JANE MONROE DONOVAN

For Bob, *still head over heels* in love with you.
And Dad, for sharing your love for all things written.

Denise

To my dad, thank you for teaching me to think *outside the box*.

Jane

Text Copyright © 2009 Denise Brennan-Nelson
Illustration Copyright © 2009 Jane Monroe Donovan

Sleeping Bear Press
310 North Main Street, Suite 300
Chelsea, MI 48118
www.sleepingbearpress.com

© 2009 Sleeping Bear Press is an imprint of Gale, a part of Cengage Learning.

Printed and bound in China.

First Edition

10 9 8 7 6 5 4 3 2 1

Library of Congress Cataloging-in-Publication Data

Brennan-Nelson, Denise.
My daddy likes to say / written by Denise Brennan-Nelson; illustrated by Jane
Monroe Donovan.
p. cm.
Summary: "Proverbs, clichés, and idioms are introduced in rhyme and illustrated
as a young child's literal interpretation. Each expression includes information
about its origin and original meaning"—Provided by publisher.
ISBN 978-1-58536-432-9
1. English language—Idioms—Juvenile literature. 2. Figures of speech—Juvenile
literature. 3. Proverbs, English—Juvenile literature. 4. Clichés—Juvenile literature.
I. Donovan, Jane Monroe, ill. II. Title.
PE1460.B724 2009
398.9'21—dc22   2008053521

Introduction

Imagine what our language would sound like without idioms, proverbs, and clichés. *Dull as dishwater*!

When I was *knee-high to a grasshopper* my daddy would say *keep it down to a roar* and a *thing of beauty is a joy forever*. Sometimes what he said *went in one ear and out the other*, but many of his words left a lasting impression on me.

While some idioms are a *dime a dozen* and some are *nothing to sneeze at*, all are an important part of our language. It can be difficult to *make heads or tails* out of idioms, but you can *bet your bottom dollar* they'll *stick around*.

Your daddy may be a *man of few words* or have the *gift of gab* but there are probably numerous expressions that your daddy likes to say.

Whatever the case may be, listen to your daddy.
And that shouldn't be a problem. After all,
everyone knows, *little pitchers have big ears*.

Does your daddy ever say things
you think are quite amusing?
Do they make you scratch your head?
Are his words a bit confusing?

I've heard him say he's a "couch potato."
Momma says so, too.
He'll say I'm a "chip off the old block"—
someday I'll "fill his shoes."

He talks about a "rat race"
and being "tied to a clock."
But Daddy's "happy as a clam"
and "crazy like a fox."

He doesn't "beat around the bush."
He'll give you the "shirt off his back."
His "bark is worse than his bite"
and he doesn't mind "cutting me slack."

I can "butter him up" at the "drop of a hat."
It's a "blessing in disguise."
And I really like when Daddy
"sees the world through my eyes."

When Daddy talks, I listen.
He might say something new.
But please don't ask me what he means
'cause I "haven't got a clue!"

 The "rat race" refers to the competitive struggle to survive in the workplace.

We "beat around the bush" when we're nervous or afraid to talk about the real subject. This expression has a hunting origin. "Beaters" would beat bushes to scare game birds from their hiding places. Others believed it referred to the hunting dog hesitating while circling a bush.

When you say a person's "bark is worse than his bite" it means they may say threatening things, but would never do threatening things. A dog may have a scary bark but that doesn't mean the dog will bite.

"Were you born in a barn?"

my daddy likes to say.
I'm not sure what he means
but I like it anyway.

I was born in a barn
with the sheep and the cattle.
A big cowbell was
was my very first rattle.

 If someone asks, "Were you born in a barn?" they are pointing out that you forgot to close the door when you came in the house.

This phrase was originally "were you born in Bardney?" Long ago after an English king was killed, his subjects tried to bring his coffin to the Bardney monastery in Lincolnshire, England, but the monks refused to open the gates. Eventually the monks were persuaded to open the monastery gates and leave them open, and the saying became "Do you come from Bardney?"

Some believe that this expression simply began because barn doors are opened in the morning to let cows out to pasture and remain open until the cows are herded back at night.

Another expression that refers to a barn is "your barn door's open." This expression lets someone know he forgot to zip his pants.

You might "bury your head in the sand" if you're trying to avoid something unpleasant. And if there are signs of danger you might want to hide your head, thinking if you don't see danger, it can't harm you.

A long time ago it was thought that an ostrich would bury its head in the sand to avoid being attacked by a predator. Some think this myth may have come about because ostrich lower their heads when feeding, which may appear as if they are burying their heads.

"Burying your head in the sand" won't make unpleasant or difficult situations go away. Instead, face them head on. Dealing with a problem may be the quickest way to "put it behind you."

If you want to bury something, "bury the hatchet." It means to bury your differences or to agree to stop arguing about something. Now that's worth burying!

Don't "bury your head in the sand,"

my daddy likes to say.
I'm not sure what he means
but I like it anyway.

Doesn't seem right,
surely everyone knows
when you bury your head
you get sand up your nose.

"Wipe that smile off your face,"

my daddy likes to say.
I'm not sure what he means
but I like it anyway.

Daddy doesn't like it
if he thinks I might be sad,
but he likes it even less
if I smile when he's mad.

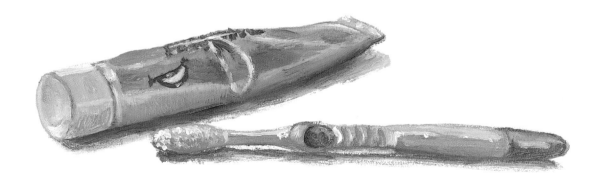

 It is not certain when or where this expression started. The interesting thing about idioms is their ability to catch on and become a lasting part of our language.

While parents prefer to see their children happy and smiling, when you have done something to upset them and you are being disciplined, it's not a good idea to be smiling. Take it from an experienced parent and "wipe that smile off your face." Save it for a more appropriate time.

You may hear this along with, "I'll send you into next week."

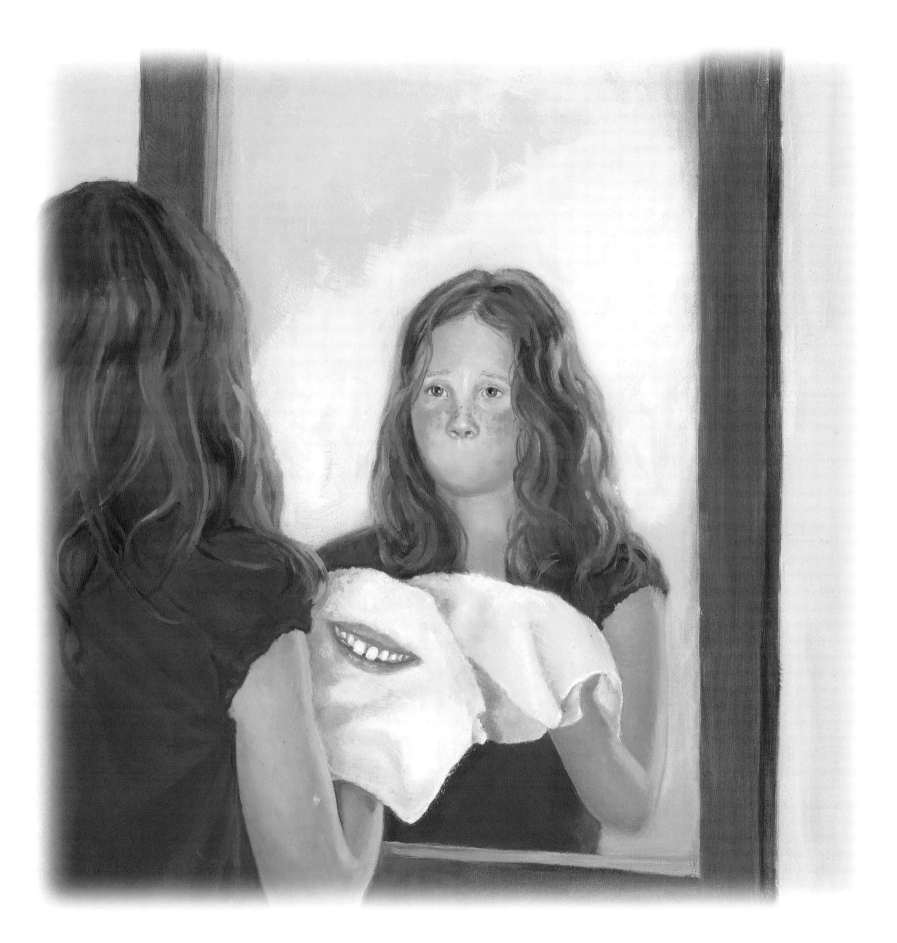

"You're coming out of your shell,"

my daddy likes to say.
I'm not sure what he means
but I like it anyway.

I crawl inside my shell
when I need somewhere to hide.
I sit and wait until I know
it's safe to come outside.

If you are "coming out of your shell," you are becoming more friendly or sociable. And if you have gone into your shell you have withdrawn or are being shy.

Some say this expression has been around since the 1500s. Back then it was referring to a baby bird emerging from its shell, and its meaning was to be young and inexperienced.

"Stick your neck out" also has a meaning involving shells. A turtle uses its shell to hide and protect itself. When a turtle sticks its neck out, it becomes vulnerable to an attack from predators.

Has there ever been a time when you have wanted to crawl into a shell?

This expression means to leave something or someone alone. If everything is calm and going well, it's best not to stir up a situation that could be dangerous or cause trouble. It was originally used in one of Geoffrey Chaucer's books: "it is nought good a slepyng hound to wake" and dates back to the 1200s. Chaucer is often named as the father of English literature.

Imagine you come upon a sleeping dog. Since you don't know how it will react if you wake it up, it's probably best to let it sleep, so it doesn't bother you when it wakes up!

"Let sleeping dogs lie,"

my daddy likes to say.
I'm not sure what he means
but I like it anyway.

The dogs were snoring loudly,
sleeping sound and deep,
so quietly I tiptoed
and never made a peep.

"Fly by the seat of your pants,"
my daddy likes to say.
I'm not sure what he means
but I like it anyway.

My seat has wings?
I never knew!
But Daddy was right
and away I flew!

This is an old aviation expression. Before airplanes had flight control systems or air traffic controllers, planes were piloted by feel. Since the largest point of contact between pilot and plane was through the "seat of his pants," that's where most of the feedback and feel came from.

If you are "flying by the seat of your pants" you are doing something by instinct, rather than by experience or instruction.

If you could "fly by the seat of your pants," where would you go?

"You're driving me up the wall,"

my daddy likes to say.
I'm not sure what he means
but I like it anyway.

We drive around the country
but my favorite trip of all
is cruising in my race car,
driving Daddy up the wall.

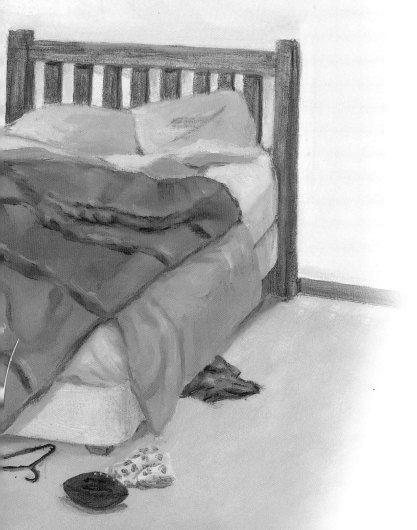

If you are "driving someone up the wall" you are frustrating or annoying them. This expression didn't originate until cars became popular in the mid-twentieth century.

To "drive" means to be in control of a situation. If someone is doing something that is annoying or making you angry, they are "driving" you to become annoyed or angry. You can also "drive" someone crazy, mad, or nuts.

Do you do anything that "drives your daddy up the wall"?

Other driving expressions: A "backseat driver" is someone who is not behind the steering wheel of a car, but wants to control the driver's actions.

If you are "in the driver's seat" you have control of a situation.

"The buck stops here,"

my daddy likes to say.
I'm not sure what he means
but I like it anyway.

He stops here and waits,
but how does he know?
We might have to tell him
it's okay to go.

 When someone wants to make it clear that he or she is taking responsibility for a situation, this expression may be used.

"The buck stops here" developed from an earlier expression, "pass the buck" which means to pass the responsibility on to someone else.

"Pass the buck" originated with the card game, poker. Many years ago a knife with a buckhorn handle was used to mark or distinguish the person who was dealing. If a person did not want to deal, they could "pass the buck," or marker on to the next player.

In his farewell speech given in January 1953, President Truman said, "The President—whoever he is—has to decide. He can't pass the buck to anybody. No one else can do the deciding for him. That's his job." In President Truman's White House office there was a sign: "The Buck Stops Here."

"Are you down in the dumps?"

"Are you down in the dumps?"
my daddy likes to say.
I'm not sure what he means
but I like it anyway.

The smell is just awful!
Stinky garbage so thick!
I'm down in the dumps.
Get me out of here quick!

 If someone is "down in the dumps" they are unhappy or sad.

When we hear this expression, we think of a garbage dump, a place where people can drop off trash or a garbage dumpster. In Shakespeare's time "in the dumps" meant out of spirits, as in feeling low or the opposite of high spirits. It was also used to refer to a slow, sad song or dance.

If you're "feeling down in the dumps," try to spend some time with someone who will "lift your spirits."

"Straight from the horse's mouth,"
my daddy likes to say.
I'm not sure what he means
but I like it anyway.

Horses can't keep secrets
and much like people, too,
the story changes greatly
by the time it gets to you!

If you get information "straight from the horse's mouth" it means that it came directly from the most reliable source.

At horse racing tracks, those closest to the horse trainers or stable hands could give some good tips on which horse is likely to win. But if someone shares information with you and says, "I got it straight from the horse's mouth" it's considered very reliable.

Another possible explanation may be the information you can get from a horse simply by looking in its mouth. By looking in a horse's mouth you can determine its age, health, and if it has ever been reined. If a horse is difficult to handle you have to pull on the reins often, which shows in the horse's mouth.

This expression has been around since the 1500s. If someone tells you that you are "cool as a cucumber," they mean you're calm and relaxed.

The inside of a cucumber can be 20 degrees cooler than the air outside the cucumber. So the next time you feel yourself getting hot or upset, think of a cucumber. It just might cool you off.

Have you ever put cucumber slices on your eyes? They are cool to the touch and can be very soothing on sore, tired eyes. Now that's cool!

"Cool as a cucumber,"

my daddy likes to say.
I'm not sure what he means
but I like it anyway.

Watch out cucumbers!
Don't be fickle.
You're not as cool
when you're a pickle.

So many odd and funny things
my daddy likes to say:
The "proof is in the pudding," and
"Rome wasn't built in a day."

We've been on a "wild goose chase."
And had a "whale of a time."
If we're not "in the doghouse"
we're sitting "on cloud nine."

And now it's time to "call it a day"
'cause all is "said and done."
I won't "pull any punches"—
My daddy's number one!

 If someone tells you you're "in the doghouse," watch out! It means that you
have done something to make them angry.

The phrase "on cloud nine" has been around since the 1930s and comes from the U.S.
Weather Bureau. At one time, the bureau rated clouds by an arithmetic sequence. The
number 9 was given to the very highest cumulonimbus clouds, the clouds that look
like mountains in the sky.

So to be "on cloud nine" means that you are at the very peak of something and
incredibly happy about being there.

Let's tie up the loose ends.

Here are a few more idioms that will help you *get a handle* on the funny things your daddy likes to say:

You're a chip off the old block if you resemble a parent in looks, personality, or behavior.

If you're *in a pickle* you are in a difficult or bad situation.

You *butter someone up* when you need help or want special treatment. Paying people compliments or flattering them is one way to *butter them up.*

If someone tells you to put some *elbow grease into it* they want you to put energy into the task and work hard.

Eat humble pie means to admit guilt.

Can't see the forest for the trees means to be so involved in the details that you don't see the whole picture.

You might *knock on wood* to keep from having bad luck, or to stop good fortune from changing to bad.

A penny for your thoughts is a way of asking someone what they are thinking about.

If your *name is mud* you have done something foolish and may be in trouble for it, or you may have a bad reputation.

To make a small issue into a big one or to make something more important than it really is, is to *make a mountain out of a molehill.*

Ace up your sleeve means you have something that will give you an advantage that others don't know about.

If you are *mad as a wet hen* you are extremely angry.

If you *cry wolf*, you are pretending that something is wrong when all is well.

When you are *on pins and needles* you are anxiously waiting for something to happen.

Out of the frying pan and into the fire means you have gone from one bad situation to another.

The *tip of the iceberg* refers to the small part of a much bigger problem.

If you're getting *too big for your britches* you think you are more important than you really are.

Shape up or ship out means to improve your behavior or attitude or leave.

If you *took the words right out of my mouth* you finished my thought for me or we are thinking alike.

I'm sure your daddy says some special things, too.

Use this page to write the things your daddy says to you.

_____

_____

_____

_____

_____

_____

_____

_____

Denise Brennan-Nelson

Denise Brennan-Nelson was raised on a small farm in Howell, Michigan with chickens, geese, sheep, cats and dogs (*the more the merrier*), six sisters, one brother, and a very large garden. It's no wonder she remembers her daddy saying, *"Keep it down to a roar."*

Denise still listens to what her daddy likes to say. And since the *apple doesn't fall far from the tree*, she now shares his *words of wisdom* with her children, Rebecca and Rachel.

This is Denise's ninth book with Sleeping Bear Press and *a little bird told us* it won't be her last! She enjoys traveling the country visiting schools, presenting workshops, and encouraging others to *follow their hearts* through writing and creativity.

She likes to *chill out* with her kids and husband, Bob, where they *live and learn* in Howell, Michigan. For more information about Denise visit www.denisebrennannelson.com.

Jane Monroe Donovan

Jane was *tickled pink* to go back to the *drawing board* when she was asked to illustrate *My Daddy Likes to Say*. The project came with *icing on the cake* since she was able to use the newest addition to her family, Tala, as a puppy model along with family dog Grizzly, who also gets his *day in the sun*. Jane has several other books *under her belt*, including the holiday favorite *Winter's Gift*, which she wrote and illustrated.

Jane is *proud as a peacock* of her sons Ryan and Joe. Although they are sometimes a *pain in the neck* they know she *has a soft spot* just for them. Her husband Bruce still makes her *heart skip a beat* and for Jane there is *no place like home*, which is in Pinckney, Michigan.